ROCK ART PAINTING

A Comprehensive Guide to Creating Stunning Rock Art Projects using various Techniques and Inspiration for Modern Artists

WILLIAM RICE
Copyright@2024

Table of Contents

Chapter 1

    ROCK ART PAINTING

    APPLICATION

    HISTORY

    Materials and tools

    TROUBLESHOOTING AND SOLUTIONS

Chapter 2

    BASIC TECHNIQUES

    INTERMEDIATE TECHNIQUES

    ADVANCED TECHNIQUES

Chapter 3

    BEGINNERS PROJECT

    INTERMEDIATE PROJECT

    Advanced project

    Conclusion

Chapter 1

ROCK ART PAINTING

Rock art painting refers to artwork created on natural rock surfaces, often found in caves or on open rock faces. This form of art includes:

1. **Petroglyphs:** Carvings or engravings made by removing parts of the rock surface.
2. **Pictographs:** Paintings or drawings made by applying pigments to the rock surface.

These artworks have been created by various cultures throughout history and often depict animals, human figures, symbols, and abstract patterns. They can provide insights into the lives, beliefs, and environments of ancient peoples. Today, rock art is studied for its historical, cultural, and artistic significance, and it continues to inspire modern artists and researchers.

APPLICATION

The application of rock art painting encompasses both practical and artistic aspects:

1. **Cultural Preservation:** Rock art serves as a historical record of past cultures, offering insights into their lives, beliefs, and practices. Preserving these artworks helps maintain cultural heritage and informs current and future generations about ancient societies.
2. **Artistic Expression:** Modern artists use rock art techniques to create unique, nature-inspired works. This includes painting or carving on rocks as a form of personal or public art, drawing from traditional methods while adding contemporary elements.
3. **Educational Purpose:** Rock art is a valuable resource for educators and researchers. It provides a hands-on way to teach about history, archaeology, and

anthropology, illustrating the development of human creativity and communication.
4. **Tourism and Recreation:** Many rock art sites are popular tourist destinations, offering people a chance to explore and appreciate ancient art. Properly managed, these sites can boost local economies while promoting respect for cultural heritage.
5. **Conservation Efforts:** Understanding the techniques used in rock art can inform conservation strategies to protect these irreplaceable artworks from environmental damage, vandalism, and other threats.
6. **Personal Projects:** For hobbyists and artists, rock art painting offers a unique medium to explore creativity. It allows for experimenting with textures, natural materials, and historical techniques in a hands-on way.

HISTORY

The history of rock art painting spans thousands of years and is a key aspect of human cultural development. Here's a brief overview:

1. **Early Beginnings (Prehistoric Era):**

   - **Origins:** Rock art is believed to date back to the Upper Paleolithic period, around 40,000 years ago. Early humans created paintings and carvings on cave walls as a form of expression or communication.
   - **Examples:** The Chauvet Cave in France and the Lascaux Cave paintings are famous early examples. These artworks often depict animals and hunting scenes, reflecting the daily life and beliefs of prehistoric peoples.

2. **Ancient Civilizations:**

   - **Neolithic and Bronze Age:** As societies transitioned from hunter-gatherers to settled agricultural communities, rock art continued to evolve. In places like the American Southwest, Africa, and Australia, rock art began to include more symbolic and ritualistic elements.
   - **Examples:** The petroglyphs of the American Southwest, the rock engravings of Africa's Sahara, and Aboriginal rock paintings in Australia all provide insights into ancient civilizations' spiritual and social practices.

3. **Classical and Medieval Periods:**

   - **Influence of Major Cultures:** As civilizations like the Egyptians, Greeks, and Romans developed, rock art began to blend with other forms of art. Although less prevalent, rock art continued to serve as a medium for depicting cultural and religious themes.
   - **Examples:** The petroglyphs of the petroglyphs of the Egyptian pyramids and the carvings found in some Roman ruins show the integration of rock art with other artistic traditions.

4. **Modern Era:**
   - **Scientific Study:** In the 19th and 20th centuries, rock art gained significant academic attention. Archaeologists and historians began to study and preserve these artworks, leading to a better understanding of their historical and cultural significance.
   - **Examples:** The discovery of the Altamira cave paintings in Spain in the late 19th century and the subsequent study of similar sites helped establish rock art as a critical field of study in archaeology.

5. **Contemporary Perspectives:**
   - **Cultural Revival:** In recent decades, there has been a renewed interest in rock art, both as a means of preserving ancient heritage and as a source of inspiration for modern artists.
- **Examples:** Efforts to protect and interpret rock art sites have increased, with many becoming protected cultural heritage sites. Additionally, contemporary artists are experimenting with rock art techniques, blending traditional methods with modern aesthetics.

Rock art continues to be an important area of study and artistic expression, offering valuable insights into the human past and inspiring new creative endeavors.

Materials and tools

Creating rock art involves specific materials and tools tailored to the medium and desired effects. Here's a guide to the materials and tools commonly used:

Materials

1. **Pigments:**
   - **Natural Pigments:** Historically, natural pigments such as ochre, charcoal, and minerals were used. These pigments can be ground and mixed with binders like animal fat or water.
   - **Synthetic Paints:** Modern artists might use acrylics or other synthetic

paints for their durability and range of colors.

2. **Binders:**
   - **Animal Fat:** Traditional binders included animal fat or other organic materials.
   - **Modern Binders:** Acrylic mediums or commercial binders can be used to mix with pigments for better adherence and longevity.

3. **Sealants:**
   - **Protective Coatings:** To preserve the artwork, especially for outdoor rock art, sealants can be applied. These might include conservation-grade sealants designed to protect the surface from weather and environmental damage.

4. **Surface Preparation Materials:**
   - **Cleaning Agents:** Gentle cleaners or brushes may be used to prepare the rock surface, ensuring it is free of dust or debris before painting.

Tools

1. **Painting Tools:**

   - **Brushes:** Various sizes of brushes, including fine-tipped ones for detailed work and larger brushes for broader strokes.

- **Sponges:** Used for applying and blending pigments, creating textures and effects.
- **Airbrushes:** For a smooth, even application of paint, though they are less traditional for rock art.

2. **Carving Tools (for petroglyphs):**

   - **Chisels:** Used for carving into the rock surface to create images or symbols.
   - **Hammers:** Paired with chisels, used to strike and shape the rock.
   - **Grinding Stones:** Used to smooth out or refine carved surfaces.

3. **Protective Gear:**

   - **Gloves:** To protect hands from pigments and abrasive materials.
   - **Masks:** To avoid inhaling dust or fumes, especially when working with powders or synthetic materials.
   - **Safety Glasses:** To protect eyes from dust and small particles.

4. **Preparation Tools:**

   - **Scrapers:** For removing loose material or old paint from rock surfaces.

- **Cleaning Brushes:** For preparing the rock surface before painting.

5. **Drawing Tools:**

- **Pencils and Chalk:** For sketching preliminary designs on the rock before painting or carving.

These materials and tools are chosen based on the specific requirements of the rock surface and the artist's desired outcome, whether creating new artwork or preserving and restoring existing rock art.

TROUBLESHOOTING AND SOLUTIONS

When working with rock art, various challenges can arise, whether you're creating new artwork or preserving existing pieces. Here are common issues and their solutions:

1. Surface Preparation Issues

Problem: Rock surface is too rough or uneven.

- **Solution:** Use grinding stones or sandpaper to smooth the surface. For extremely rough surfaces, you may need to use a combination of tools to achieve a workable texture.

Problem: Dust or debris on the surface affecting paint adhesion.

- **Solution:** Clean the surface thoroughly with brushes or gentle cleaners. Ensure the surface is completely dry before applying paint.

2. Paint Application Problems

Problem: Paint doesn't adhere properly.

- **Solution:** Ensure the rock surface is clean and dry. Use appropriate binders to mix with pigments for better adhesion. Consider using a primer or base coat if the surface is particularly porous.

Problem: Colors appear faded or uneven.

- **Solution:** Apply multiple layers of paint for more vibrant colors. After each coat has dried, apply the next. Use a consistent technique for applying and blending paints.

3. Pigment and Binder Issues

Problem: Natural pigments are not mixing well or are inconsistent.

- **Solution:** Ensure pigments are finely ground and thoroughly mixed with the binder. If necessary, use a sieve to remove larger particles.

Problem: Synthetic paints are not adhering to the rock.

- **Solution:** Ensure the paint is designed for use on porous surfaces. Apply a primer or adhesion promoter before painting.

4. Environmental and Weather Challenges

Problem: Artwork is deteriorating due to weather exposure.

- **Solution:** Apply a conservation-grade sealant to protect the artwork from environmental damage. For outdoor artworks, consider installing protective coverings or shelters.

Problem: Moss or lichen growth on painted surfaces.

- **Solution:** Gently clean the surface with a soft brush or mild cleaner. Avoid harsh chemicals that could damage the paint or rock. Regular maintenance can help prevent growth.

5. Carving Issues

Problem: Carving tools are not working effectively.

- **Solution:** Ensure tools are sharp and appropriate for the rock type. For harder rocks, use specialized chisels and hammers designed for tough materials.

Problem: Carvings are becoming damaged or eroded.

- **Solution:** Protect carvings with a sealant. To keep the surface in good condition, stay away from harsh cleaning products.

6. Preservation and Restoration

Problem: Existing rock art is fading or deteriorating.

- **Solution:** Consult with conservation experts to assess the condition and recommend appropriate treatments. Preservation techniques might include cleaning, sealing, and controlled environmental conditions.

Problem: Damage from vandalism or neglect.

- **Solution:** Report damage to appropriate authorities or conservation groups. Restoration might involve careful cleaning, repainting, or even reconstructing damaged areas under professional guidance.

By addressing these issues with the right solutions, you can ensure that rock art remains vibrant and preserved, whether you're working on new projects or caring for historical pieces.

Chapter 2

BASIC TECHNIQUES

Here's a step-by-step guide to three basic rock art techniques, including the materials needed for each:

1. Pictograph (Painting)

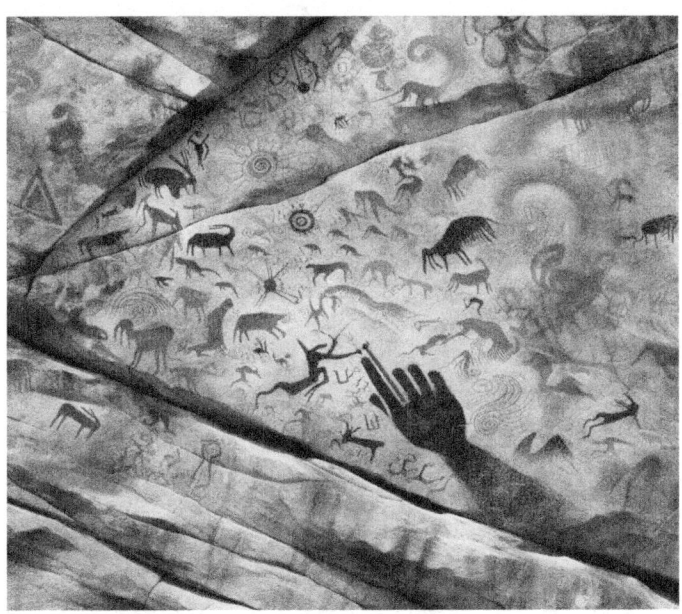

Materials Needed:

- Natural or synthetic pigments (e.g., ochre, charcoal, acrylic paints)
- Binders (e.g., animal fat, acrylic medium)

- Brushes (various sizes)
- Sponges or cloths
- Water or solvents (depending on the binder)
- Sealant (optional, for protection)

Steps:

1. **Preparation:**

   - Clean the rock surface with a brush to remove dirt and debris.
   - Ensure the surface is dry before starting.

2. **Mixing Pigments:**

   - Grind natural pigments into a fine powder if using them.
   - Mix the pigment with a binder (e.g., animal fat or acrylic medium) to create paint. Adjust the consistency with water or solvent if needed.

3. **Sketching:**

   - Lightly sketch your design on the rock with a pencil or chalk.

4. **Painting:**

   - Use brushes to apply the paint to the rock. Start with a base layer and build up color as needed.

- Use sponges or cloths for blending or creating textures.

5. **Finishing:**

   - Allow the paint to dry completely.
   - Apply a sealant if desired to protect the artwork from the elements.

2. Petroglyph (Carving)

Materials Needed:

- Chisels (various sizes)
- Hammers
- Safety goggles and gloves
- Pencil or chalk for sketching

Steps:

1. **Preparation:**

   - Clean the rock surface to remove any loose material.
   - Wear safety goggles and gloves for protection.

2. **Sketching:**

   - Lightly sketch your design on the rock with a pencil or chalk.

3. **Carving:**

   - Use a chisel and hammer to carefully carve the design into the rock. Start with light taps and gradually deepen the carving.
   - Work from the edges inward to maintain control over the carving depth and detail.

4. **Refining:**

   - Use smaller chisels or tools to refine details and smooth out rough edges.
   - Clean the carving with a soft brush to remove any debris.

5. **Preservation:**

   - Apply a protective sealant if necessary, especially for outdoor or exposed carvings.

3. Stenciling

Materials Needed:

- Stencil templates (made from plastic or cardboard)
- Natural or synthetic paints
- Brushes or sponges
- Painter's tape or adhesive (optional)

Steps:

1. **Preparation:**

- Clean the rock surface to ensure good adhesion of the stencil and paint.

- Position your stencil on the rock. Use painter's tape or adhesive to secure it if needed.

2. **Painting:**

   - Apply paint using a brush or sponge over the stencil. Dab gently to avoid paint bleeding under the stencil edges.
   - Use contrasting colors for better visibility.

3. **Removing the Stencil:**

   - To prevent smearing, remove the stencil carefully while the paint is still wet.

4. **Finishing:**

   - Allow the paint to dry completely.
   - Apply a sealant if desired to protect the artwork.

These techniques offer different ways to create rock art, each with its unique process and effect. Choose the technique that best fits your artistic vision and the rock surface you're working with.

INTERMEDIATE TECHNIQUES

Here are step-by-step guides for two intermediate rock art techniques, along with the materials needed for each:

1. Layered Paint Technique

Materials Needed:

- Natural or synthetic pigments
- Binders (e.g., acrylic medium, animal fat)
- Brushes (various sizes)
- Sponges or cloths
- Water or solvents (for adjusting paint consistency)
- Palette or mixing surface
- Sealant (optional, for protection)

Steps:

1. **Preparation:**

   - Clean the rock surface thoroughly with a brush to remove dirt and debris. Ensure the surface is completely dry.

2. **Base Layer:**

   - Mix your base color with a binder to achieve the desired consistency. Apply a thin, even layer of paint to the rock surface using a large brush or sponge.
   - Before moving on, make sure the base layer is fully dry.

3. **Adding Layers:**

   - Mix additional colors for the subsequent layers. Ensure each color is slightly different in opacity or hue to create depth.
   - Apply the second layer of paint over the base layer. Use a brush or sponge to blend colors if needed, working from light to dark shades.
   - Continue layering until the desired effect is achieved. Do not apply additional layers until the previous ones have dried.

4. **Detailing:**

    - Once the layers are dry, add finer details with a small brush or sponge. This can include textures, patterns, or highlights.

5. **Finishing:**

    - Allow the artwork to dry completely.
    - Apply a sealant if desired to protect the painting from environmental factors.

2. Textured Paint Technique

Materials Needed:

- Natural or synthetic paints (e.g., acrylics)
- Texturing agents (e.g., sand, modeling paste, gel medium)
- Brushes (various sizes)
- Palette or mixing surface
- Sponges or cloths
- Sealant (optional, for protection)

Steps:

1. **Preparation:**

   - Clean the rock surface to remove any loose material. Ensure it is dry before starting.

2. **Mixing Texture Medium:**

   - In a mixing bowl or palette, combine your paint with a texturing agent. For example, mix sand or modeling paste with acrylic paint to create texture.
   - Adjust the consistency to your liking; thicker mixtures will provide more pronounced textures.

3. **Applying the Base Texture:**

   - Apply the textured paint mixture to the rock using a brush or palette knife. Create patterns or textures as

desired. For a more pronounced texture, use a thicker layer.
- Allow this base layer to dry completely before adding additional textures.

4. **Building Up Layers:**

   - Add more layers of textured paint if desired, using different texturing agents or techniques to create depth and variation.
   - For added effect, use a sponge or cloth to dab and blend different textures.

5. **Detailing:**

   - Once the textured base is dry, add finer details or highlights using regular paint. This helps to emphasize the textures and add dimension.

6. **Finishing:**

   - Allow the artwork to dry thoroughly.
   - Apply a sealant if needed to protect the textured paint from weathering and damage.

Both of these intermediate techniques offer a way to add complexity and depth to rock art, creating visually interesting and durable artworks.

ADVANCED TECHNIQUES

Here are step-by-step guides for two advanced rock art techniques, along with the materials needed for each:

1. Mosaic Rock Art

Materials Needed:

- Small stones, glass, or ceramic tiles (for mosaics)
- Adhesive (e.g., tile adhesive, glue)
- Grout (for filling gaps)
- Tools (e.g., tweezers, spatula, sponge)
- Sealant (optional, for protection)
- Base rock or substrate (if creating a mosaic on a separate surface)

Steps:

1. **Preparation:**

   - Clean the base rock or substrate thoroughly to ensure good adhesion of the mosaic pieces.
   - If working with a rock directly, ensure it is dry and free of debris.

2. **Design Layout:**

   - Plan your mosaic design on paper or use a digital design tool. Arrange the stones or tiles on the rock or substrate to visualize the pattern.

3. **Adhering Pieces:**

   - Apply adhesive to the back of each mosaic piece and press them onto the rock or substrate according to your design. Use tweezers for precision placement.
   - After applying the glue, let it dry as directed by the manufacturer.

4. **Grouting:**

   - Once the adhesive is fully dry, apply grout over the mosaic pieces using a spatula or grout float. Ensure the grout fills all the gaps between the pieces.

- Wipe off excess grout with a damp sponge before it sets, taking care not to remove grout from between the pieces.

5. **Finishing:**

- Let the grout dry completely.
- Apply a sealant if desired to protect the mosaic from environmental damage.

2. Relief Sculpture

Materials Needed:

- Modeling clay or plaster (for creating the relief)
- Sculpting tools (e.g., carving tools, spatulas)

- Adhesive (if attaching the relief to a rock)
- Paints (for adding color and details)
- Sealant (optional, for protection)

Steps:

1. **Preparation:**

   - Clean the rock surface thoroughly. If creating a relief on a separate substrate, prepare that surface as needed.

2. **Design and Sculpting:**

   - Sketch your design on the rock or substrate. If using modeling clay or plaster, build up the base layer of the relief according to your design.
   - Use sculpting tools to refine the details of the relief, creating textures and patterns.

3. **Drying:**

   - Allow the clay or plaster to dry completely. This may take several hours to a few days, depending on the material and thickness.

4. **Attachment (if applicable):**

   - If you created the relief separately from the rock, use adhesive to attach it to the rock or substrate. Ensure it is securely fixed and allow the adhesive to set.

5. **Painting and Detailing:**

- Paint the relief with acrylic or other suitable paints. Add details and highlights to enhance the texture and depth of the sculpture.

6. **Finishing:**

- Once the paint is dry, apply a sealant if desired to protect the relief from environmental damage.

These advanced techniques offer opportunities to create detailed and dynamic rock art that incorporates texture, color, and intricate designs.

Chapter 3

BEGINNERS PROJECT

Here are step-by-step instructions for seven beginner rock art projects, along with the materials needed for each.

1. Painted Rock Animals

Materials Needed:

- Smooth, clean rocks

- Acrylic paints
- Paintbrushes (various sizes)
- Water cup (for cleaning brushes)
- Paper towels or cloth (for drying brushes)
- Sealant (optional)

Steps:

1. **Preparation:**

    - Clean the rocks with water and let them dry completely.

2. **Design:**

    - Sketch your animal design lightly on the rock with a pencil.

3. **Painting:**

    - Use acrylic paints and brushes to fill in the design. Start with base colors and add details as you go.

4. **Finishing:**

    - Allow the paint to dry completely. Apply a sealant if desired to protect the design.

2. Dot Painting

Materials Needed:

- Smooth, clean rocks
- Acrylic paints
- Tools for dotting or the tip of a paintbrush
- Water cup (for cleaning tools)
- Paper towels or cloth (for drying)
- Sealant (optional)

Steps:

1. **Preparation:**
   - Clean and dry the rocks.
2. **Design:**
   - Plan your dot pattern. You can create simple geometric shapes or more intricate designs.
3. **Painting:**
   - Dip your dotting tool into paint and apply dots in your chosen pattern on the rock.
4. **Finishing:**
   - Let the paint dry completely. Apply a sealant for durability.

3. Inspirational Quotes

Materials Needed:

- Smooth, clean rocks
- Acrylic paints
- Paintbrushes
- Pencil
- Water cup (for cleaning brushes)
- Paper towels or cloth
- Sealant (optional)

Steps:

1. **Preparation:**

   - Clean and dry the rocks.

2. **Design:**

   - Sketch the quote lightly on the rock with a pencil.

3. **Painting:**

   - Paint over the pencil sketch using a fine brush. Add decorative elements if desired.

4. **Finishing:**

   - Allow the paint to dry. Apply a sealant if desired.

4. Abstract Patterns

Materials Needed:

- Smooth, clean rocks
- Acrylic paints
- Paintbrushes and sponges
- Water cup (for cleaning)
- Paper towels or cloth
- Sealant (optional)

Steps:

1. **Preparation:**

   - Clean and dry the rocks.

2. **Design:**

   - Plan your abstract pattern. It can be a series of shapes or random patterns.

3. **Painting:**

   - Use brushes or sponges to apply paint in various patterns and colors.

4. **Finishing:**

   - Let the paint dry. Apply a sealant if needed.

5. Rock Garden Markers

Materials Needed:

- Smooth, clean rocks
- Acrylic paints
- Paintbrushes
- Pencil
- Water cup (for cleaning)
- Paper towels or cloth
- Sealant (optional)

Steps:

1. **Preparation:**

    - Clean and dry the rocks.

2. **Design:**

    - Write or draw garden labels or designs on the rocks with a pencil.
3. **Painting:**

    - Paint the labels or designs using acrylic paints.
4. **Finishing:**

    - Allow the paint to dry completely. Apply a sealant for protection.

6. Simple Nature Scenes

Materials Needed:

- Smooth, clean rocks
- Acrylic paints
- Paintbrushes
- Pencil

- Water cup (for cleaning)
- Paper towels or cloth
- Sealant (optional)

Steps:

1. **Preparation:**

   - Clean and dry the rocks.
2. **Design:**

   - Sketch a simple nature scene (e.g., a tree, sunset, or flowers) on the rock.
3. **Painting:**

   - Paint the scene with acrylic paints, starting with background colors and adding details.
4. **Finishing:**

   - Allow the paint to dry. Apply a sealant if desired.

7. Seasonal Themes

Materials Needed:

- Smooth, clean rocks
- Acrylic paints
- Paintbrushes
- Pencil
- Water cup (for cleaning)
- Paper towels or cloth
- Sealant (optional)

Steps:

1. **Preparation:**

   - Clean and dry the rocks.

2. **Design:**

   - Sketch a seasonal theme (e.g., autumn leaves, winter snowflakes) on the rock.

3. **Painting:**

   - Paint the seasonal theme using acrylic paints.

4. **Finishing:**

   - Let the paint dry. Apply a sealant if desired.

These beginner projects are designed to help you get started with rock art, providing a range of simple yet creative ideas.

INTERMEDIATE PROJECT

Here are step-by-step guides for four intermediate rock art projects, along with the materials needed for each.

1. Rock Mandalas

Materials Needed:

- Smooth, clean rocks
- Acrylic paints
- Tools for dotting or the tip of a paintbrush
- Pencil (for sketching)
- Water cup (for cleaning tools)
- Paper towels or cloth (for drying)
- Sealant (optional)

Steps:

1. **Preparation:**

    - Clean and dry the rocks thoroughly.

2. **Design:**

   - Lightly sketch a mandala pattern on the rock with a pencil. Mandalas often consist of concentric circles and patterns radiating outward.

3. **Base Layer:**

   - Apply a base color to the rock using a larger brush. Allow it to dry completely.

4. **Dotting:**

   - Using Tools for dotting or the tip of a paintbrush, start applying dots and small details according to your mandala design. Begin from the center and work outward, layering colors and creating patterns.

5. **Finishing:**

   - Let the paint dry completely. Apply a sealant if desired to protect the mandala.

2. Rock Garden Decor with Textured Patterns

Materials Needed:

- Smooth, clean rocks
- Modeling paste or textured gel medium
- Acrylic paints
- Paintbrushes
- Palette or mixing surface
- Sculpting tools (e.g., palette knife)
- Water cup (for cleaning)
- Paper towels or cloth
- Sealant (optional)

Steps:

1. **Preparation:**

   - Clean and dry the rocks. Prepare your workspace with modeling paste or textured gel medium.

2. **Applying Texture:**

   - Apply a layer of modeling paste or gel medium to the rock using a palette knife or brush. Create patterns or textures, such as swirls or raised designs.

3. **Drying:**

   - Allow the textured layer to dry completely.

4. **Painting:**

   - Paint over the textured surface with acrylic paints. Use different colors and techniques to highlight the textures.

5. **Finishing:**

   - Let the paint dry completely. Apply a sealant to protect the textured paint.

3. Stenciled Rock Art

Materials Needed:

- Smooth, clean rocks
- Stencil templates (plastic or cardboard)
- Acrylic paints
- Paintbrushes or sponges
- Painter's tape (optional)
- Water cup (for cleaning)
- Paper towels or cloth
- Sealant (optional)

Steps:

1. **Preparation:**

   - Clean and dry the rocks. Position your stencil on the rock. Use painter's tape to secure the stencil if needed.

2. **Applying Paint:**

   - Apply paint over the stencil using a brush or sponge. Dab gently to avoid paint bleeding under the stencil edges.

3. **Removing the Stencil:**

   - To prevent smudging, carefully remove the stencil while paint is still wet.

4. **Finishing:**

   - Allow the paint to dry completely. Apply a sealant if desired.

4. Rock Art Collages

Materials Needed:

- Smooth, clean rocks
- Small pebbles, glass pieces, or tiles
- Adhesive (e.g., tile adhesive or glue)
- Grout (optional, for filling gaps)
- Paints (optional, for background or details)
- Sculpting tools (for detailed placement)
- Sealant (optional)

Steps:

1. **Preparation:**

   - Clean and dry the rocks. Arrange your small pebbles, glass pieces, or tiles to plan your collage design.

2. **Adhering Pieces:**

   - Apply adhesive to the back of each piece and place them onto the rock according to your design. Press firmly and allow the adhesive to set.

3. **Grouting (optional):**

   - Once the adhesive is dry, apply grout over the pieces to fill any gaps. Use a spatula or grout float and wipe off excess grout with a damp sponge.

4. **Painting (optional):**

   - Paint around the mosaic pieces if you wish to add background color or details.

5. **Finishing:**

   - Allow everything to dry completely. Apply a sealant if desired to protect the rock art.

These intermediate projects introduce more complex techniques and allow for creative expression while building on foundational skills in rock art.

Advanced project

Here are step-by-step guides for three advanced rock art projects, along with the materials needed for each:

1. Rock Art Relief Sculptures

Materials Needed:

- Large, smooth rocks or a sturdy base (e.g., wooden board)

- Modeling clay, plaster, or polymer clay
- Sculpting tools (e.g., carving tools, spatulas)
- Paints (acrylic or oil-based)
- Paintbrushes
- Sealant (optional)

Steps:

1. **Preparation:**

   - Clean and dry the rock or base surface thoroughly.

2. **Design:**

   - Sketch your relief sculpture design on paper. Transfer the design to the rock using a pencil.

3. **Building the Relief:**

   - Apply a base layer of modeling clay or plaster to the rock, building up the forms according to your design. Use sculpting tools to shape and refine the details.

4. **Drying:**

   - Allow the clay or plaster to dry completely, according to the manufacturer's instructions.

5. **Painting:**

- Once dry, paint the relief with acrylic or oil-based paints. Apply base colors first, then add highlights and details.

6. **Finishing:**

    - Allow the paint to dry. Apply a sealant if desired to protect the sculpture.

2. Multi-layered Rock Mosaics

Materials Needed:

- Large, clean rocks or a sturdy base
- Small mosaic tiles (glass, ceramic, or stone)
- Adhesive (tile adhesive or strong glue)
- Grout
- Grouting tools (e.g., spatula or grout float)
- Paints (for background or details, optional)
- Sealant (optional)

Steps:

1. **Preparation:**

   - Clean and dry the rock or base. Plan your mosaic design.

2. **Design Layout:**

   - Arrange the mosaic tiles on the rock according to your design. Adjust the placement as needed.

3. **Adhering Tiles:**

   - Apply adhesive to the back of each tile and press them onto the rock or base. Ensure each piece is firmly attached.

4. **Grouting:**

   - Once the adhesive is dry, apply grout over the mosaic tiles, filling gaps between them. Use a spatula or grout float to spread and smooth the grout.

5. **Cleaning:**

   - Use a moist sponge to remove any excess grout before it sets. Let the grout cure entirely.

6. **Painting and Finishing (optional):**

   - Paint around the tiles if you want to add background colors or details.

Apply a sealant to protect the mosaic if desired.

3. Inlay Rock Art with Semi-precious Stones

Materials Needed:

- Smooth rocks with a suitable surface
- Semi-precious stones or gems
- Epoxy resin or strong adhesive
- Sculpting tools (for creating cavities)
- Paints (optional, for background or details)
- Sealant (optional)

Steps:

1. **Preparation:**

   - Clean and dry the rocks. Plan your design and prepare the semi-precious stones.

2. **Creating Cavities:**

   - Use sculpting tools to carefully carve out cavities or recesses in the rock where the semi-precious stones will be inlaid.

3. **Placing Stones:**

   - Apply epoxy resin or strong adhesive to the cavities and place the semi-precious stones into the recesses. Ensure they are securely fixed.

4. **Finishing:**

   - Follow the manufacturer's directions for how long the adhesive needs to set. Optionally, paint around the stones to enhance the design.
   - Apply a sealant if desired to protect the artwork.

These advanced projects require more intricate techniques and materials but offer the opportunity to create highly detailed and striking rock art pieces.

TIPS FOR SUCCESS

Here are some tips for success when working on advanced rock art projects:

1. Plan and Design Thoroughly

- **Sketch First:** Create detailed sketches or digital designs before starting. This helps visualize the final piece and plan your approach.
- **Test Materials:** Test paints, adhesives, and other materials on a small sample rock to ensure compatibility and desired effects.

2. Prepare Your Workspace

- **Clean Environment:** Ensure your workspace is clean and well-organized. Protect surfaces and work in a well-ventilated area, especially when using adhesives or paints.
- **Proper Tools:** Use the right tools for each stage of the project. Investing in quality sculpting tools and brushes can make a significant difference.

3. Take Your Time

- **Allow for Drying:** Ensure each layer of paint, adhesive, or grout is fully

dry before proceeding to the next step. Rushing can lead to smudging or incomplete adhesion.
- **Work in Stages:** Break the project into manageable stages. This approach allows you to focus on each detail without feeling overwhelmed.

4. Handle Materials with Care

- **Precision:** Be precise when applying adhesives, grouting, or painting to avoid mistakes and ensure a clean finish.
- **Safety:** Follow safety instructions for all materials, especially when using chemicals or sharp tools. Wear protective gear as needed.

5. Maintain Detail and Quality

- **Detail Work:** Pay attention to fine details, especially in relief sculptures and mosaics. Use fine brushes and small tools for intricate work.
- **Consistent Technique:** Maintain a consistent technique for painting and applying textures. This guarantees consistency and an air of professionalism.

6. Protect and Preserve

- **Sealant Application:** Apply a sealant to protect your artwork from weathering and damage, especially for outdoor projects.
- **Storage:** Store completed rocks in a safe place to avoid chipping or scratching. If displaying outdoors, consider protective measures.

7. Learn and Adapt

- **Practice:** Practice techniques on smaller or less critical projects to build confidence and skill.
- **Adapt Techniques:** Be willing to adapt your techniques based on the materials and the unique challenges of each project.

8. Seek Feedback

- **Feedback:** Submit your work to others and ask for their honest opinions. This can provide valuable insights and help you improve your skills.
- **Community:** Engage with rock art communities online or locally to exchange tips and inspiration.

Following these tips can help ensure that your advanced rock art projects are successful and rewarding, resulting in beautiful and durable creations.

ADDING EMBELLISHMENTS

Adding embellishments to rock art can enhance the visual appeal and add unique details to your projects. Here's a guide on how to incorporate various embellishments into your rock art:

1. Using Semi-Precious Stones and Gems

Materials Needed:

- Semi-precious stones or gems
- Epoxy resin or strong adhesive
- Sculpting tools (for creating cavities)

Steps:

1. **Design and Placement:**
    - Plan where you want to place the stones or gems on your rock. Sketch the design if necessary.
2. **Creating Cavities:**
    - Carve small cavities into the rock where the stones will be

set. Ensure the cavities are slightly larger than the stones to accommodate the adhesive.
3. **Adhering Stones:**
   - Apply epoxy resin or adhesive to the cavities and place the stones firmly into the adhesive. Let it cure according to the directions on the packaging.
4. **Finishing Touches:**
   - Clean off any excess adhesive around the stones once it's dried. Optionally, paint or seal around the stones for additional protection.

2. Incorporating Beads and Sequins

Materials Needed:

- Beads, sequins, or small decorative elements
- Adhesive (e.g., glue or epoxy)
- Tweezers (for precise placement)

Steps:

1. **Plan Your Design:**

- Decide on the placement and arrangement of beads or sequins.

Arrange them on your rock to visualize the design.

2. **Adhering Embellishments:**

   - Apply a small amount of adhesive to the rock where each bead or sequin will go. Use tweezers to place the embellishments accurately.

3. **Drying:**

   - Allow the adhesive to dry completely before handling the rock.

4. **Sealing:**

   - Optionally, apply a sealant over the entire rock to protect the beads or sequins from damage.

3. Adding Metal or Wire Accents

Materials Needed:

- Thin metal wire or metal accents
- Wire cutters
- Adhesive or soldering equipment (if needed)

Steps:

1. **Design and Cutting:**

   - Plan your design and cut the metal wire or accents to the desired lengths or shapes.

2. **Attaching Metal:**

   - Use adhesive to attach the metal wire or accents to the rock. For more permanent installations, consider soldering.

3. **Finishing:**

   - Ensure all metal pieces are securely attached and allow any adhesive or solder to set completely.

4. **Using Textured Paints and Mediums**

Materials Needed:

- Textured paint mediums (e.g., modeling paste, gel medium)
- Acrylic paints
- Paintbrushes and palette knives

Steps:

1. **Apply Textured Medium:**

   - Mix your textured medium with paint or apply it directly to the rock where you want to add texture. Use a palette knife or brush to create patterns and effects.

2. **Drying:**

   - Allow the textured paint to dry completely.

3. **Painting and Detailing:**

   - Once dry, you can paint over the textured areas to add color and highlight details.

5. Incorporating Nature Elements

Materials Needed:

- Natural elements (e.g., small shells, leaves, twigs)
- Adhesive (e.g., glue or epoxy)
- Paints (optional)

Steps:

1. **Design and Arrangement:**

- Arrange the natural elements on the rock to find a pleasing design.
2. **Adhering Natural Elements:**

- Apply adhesive to the rock and press the natural elements into place.
3. **Finishing:**

- Allow the adhesive to dry completely. Optionally, paint or seal around the natural elements to integrate them into the rock art.

General Tips for Adding Embellishments:

- **Test Adhesives:** Always test adhesives on a small area or scrap piece to ensure compatibility with your rock and embellishments.
- **Precision:** Use small tools and tweezers for precise placement of tiny embellishments.
- **Sealing:** Consider applying a clear sealant over your entire rock art piece to protect embellishments and enhance durability.
- **Maintenance:** Regularly check for any loose embellishments and reattach them as needed.

Adding embellishments can significantly enhance your rock art, making it more vibrant and unique.

Conclusion

Creating rock art is a rewarding and creative endeavor that allows you to transform simple stones into beautiful, expressive works of art. Whether you're a beginner or an experienced artist, each project offers opportunities to explore various techniques and materials, enhancing your skills and creativity.

Keywords:

- **Diverse Techniques:** From basic painted designs to intricate mosaics and relief sculptures, there are endless ways to personalize and elevate your rock art. Starting with simple projects builds foundational skills, while more advanced techniques, such as incorporating semi-precious stones or textured mediums, offer a chance to showcase your artistic flair.
- **Attention to Detail:** Success in rock art often hinges on careful planning and attention to detail. Preparing your materials, taking your time with each

step, and ensuring thorough drying and finishing will contribute to the durability and beauty of your artwork.
- **Creativity and Experimentation:** Don't be afraid to experiment with different materials and embellishments. Each rock presents a unique canvas, and exploring various methods can lead to surprising and delightful results.
- **Preservation and Protection:** Applying sealants and protecting your artwork from environmental damage ensures longevity and maintains the integrity of your designs.

Rock art is not just about the final piece but also about the process of creating and enjoying your artistic journey. Embrace the process, learn from each project, and continue to experiment and refine your techniques. With practice and patience, you'll create stunning rock art that reflects your personal style and creativity.

Printed in Dunstable, United Kingdom